Any Closer to Home

poems by

Katie Daley

Finishing Line Press
Georgetown, Kentucky

Any Closer to Home

Publisher: Leah Huete de Maines
Editor: Christen Kincaid
Cover Art: Tom Daley: "Blue Ridges. After a photo by Callie Warner."
Author Photo: Laura Anne Kulber Mintz
Cover Design: Katie Daley

Order online: www.finishinglinepress.com
                also available on amazon.com

Author inquiries and mail orders:
Finishing Line Press
PO Box 1626
Georgetown, Kentucky 40324
USA

Table of Contents

for John Earl, who gets me where I live
and for all of us

Artists' Lullaby

The last day on earth,
I plucked some muddy blues
while you glued moonstones to a broken mirror
that can't ever come together again,
shards that won't ever spend their crumpled tin
on any who or what again.
Fixing to make that shatter give up a glimmer,
you went ahead and drizzled a river
from a can of sand. Aren't you something,
giving a go at the hands of God?
And don't I have some nerve, bawling the blues
when I lived with the likes of you?
Aw, hell, if I had a dime
for all the everything we busted
on what can't be fixed,
all the nothing we were fixing to lose.
It's all right, baby. The world was crumpling,
and we were wondering what the hell we could do
with six strings and a bottle of glue.
You with your hands wandering the shimmer,
me with my voice traveling the throat.
But isn't that some way to love somebody
on the last day on earth?
Don't fret about it anymore.
We did what we could.
We worked in the dark, baby.
We gave what we had.

2020

I asked the blithe guides & growling stones
from all corners of the cosmos
how would or could or should I ever
mute the mumbling blare
of inner rills & world asunder

& they said: You & the world
are an oboe
up in hiccups & flames
Be wide, be sky
Send wind cool like mint
through holy tone holes
& the rock in you
that dozes in the sun
Come nightfall the id will still
plumb its whammy
& ocean still
flint back at the moon
musing & singing & saying
even this trouble is a song

Bring it

Somebody shrieks there's a black heart in your world
and you think, yeah, that's right, black as the bottom of the sea
before Jacques Cousteau started snooping around down there
with his French accent and waterproof flashlight

and maybe it's a dangerous heart, maybe it's a lucky black
churning with wild guesses and everything we've never known
and we don't have to, but when we live on the crumbled side
of town we think, what the hell, might as well

drink deep, it's what we've got, don't need no aqua lung
to cradle our breath while we skim our heels
        across the black holes
between one star and the next, we know our wooly wise
won't dim down out there if we fall in when the batteries go dead,

we know dead and what comes after dead, we know
        dark and what's
deeper than dark, yeah, that's right, this is bottomland, other side
of the moon broken black coral land, cow shit
        and shat-out seed land,
this is the downside up upside down part of town, welcome to it,

bring your black heart, your dangerous heart,
your wild heart, drink deep

Frank the Dog's Walking Meditation for His Minders
after Ellen Bass

I smell what you're thinking.
And you might be right—
hair-raising things are bound to happen.
Winter will surely come. Black ice
could take your wheel.
The green dollar bills you capture prey with
might lose their teeth.
Already the West in flames, the South swollen
with hurricanes and trash. One day,
a gang of two-leggeds
reeking of gunpowder
might knock on our door, paste signs
over our windows, force us out
of the cozy brick house we currently curl up in.
No matter what, someday,
your body will be buried six feet under a stone
or tossed like an empty carton of Milk Bones
into the fire. Mine too. But here's the thing.
Right here, right now, out in this bitter freeze,
snowflakes are landing on my midnight pelt
in the shape of the Milky Way. Take off
your gloves. Come kneel down beside me
in this white light pulled down from the sky.
Swirl your hands across my back and scoop the stars
into your palms. Feed them to me. Feed them to you.
Let's drink the constellations till we're slaked,
till there's enough fire shaken from the cosmos
for it to fill its own cup and drink, too.

Distance Kept

inspired by Stephen Yusko's sculpture, "Sanctuary, Here to There"

We set out with one mast, no sail, and a boil of pirates,
a rope of hunger flung to the curve of the earth.
Every yesterday was a vessel sunk in the dusk behind us,
home a flotilla of worn-out dress shoes gone up in flame.
We cast passage from the smoke
and bet on the stars, the sea with its sad, onion breath.
Dolphins cruised past, hungover and indifferent.
Now and then a foghorn moaned, not for us,
but for someone's lost dog, a braid snipped from the scalp,
a mitten in the mud. There was one spoon
and no porridge. A boatload of splayed hands.
We may as well have been sweeping
the front stoop of Jupiter, which anyone would tell you
was never ours to sweep. We used to dream
of mathematics and revolutions
but now all we wanted was a place
made of cooled magma and cello notes
where it might be safe
to settle and rust and flake and fail.
Someplace on the outskirts of town
where nobody would mind if the light there
shone from within us or without.

Migrant

This will be the season when you are afraid. When you gather apples under dark skies. The era when day after day, in the shadow of a volcano, you will be obliged to scurry back and forth as you fill crater-sized bins with fruit bound for hands you will never grasp, tongues whose thoughts you will never hear. Locals will tell you the volcano is dead. They will be wrong.

It will be the season of the bossman. The season to hide the bruises, to fill your pockets and stuff your mouth with bruises. When you part your lips to confide in your fellow pickers, the rotten bits will spill out, and your comrades will look carefully away. They will comment to each other then about the snow on the higher reaches of the volcano, how they can see it glimmering all the way from here.

This will be the chapter in your life when you are allotted a one-room cabin with a wood stove and a pile of wood. When you have no choice but to build a fire. When you finally apprehend the finiteness of a flame. How you'll be forced to master the art of starting up, again and again, from the world's endings. The discarded papers, the felled trees, the fallen stars.

A fellow picker will show you how to stand a log on its feet and aim a hatchet at its head. Blow after blow, you will discover that the knots won't give way. Not to the blade of loss, not to the grunt of sorrow, not to the heave of need. Morning after morning, you will rise from sleep and have nothing more than splinters and black moons to feed to the cold.

It will be different with the volcano. Each time you glance up from your work and peer through the gnarled branches, green leaves and red fruit, there it will be. Immense, blue, a shawl of ancient snow. You will be struck, as if it's dropped a stone from a star into the bottom of you. As if it's purled one lone ripple across the scrim of your life. In that moment, you'll understand there is no longer any need to be recognized because you never truly went away. In the next moment, you will have gone irrevocably away.

Amidst all this, there will be a donkey that grazes somewhere in the valley. Each time it bellows its mournful protest, it will feel more a part of you than your own hand that reaches to pluck apple after apple after apple in the shadow of a volcano that you know is only still, not dead. Of all that has passed, this is the thing of which you are most certain.

Premonition

for John Earl

Those years, I slept alone under a concert grand piano.
It had never been splintered or warped by the weather,
and was always in perfect tune. I barely played it.
There was a tiny porch off the kitchen
where the landlord had nailed chicken wire on all sides
to keep out the pigeons and their shit. I stood there every morning
and tried to weigh down the wagon of time
by murmuring *hello* to the world: whir of traffic, cold rain,
worms in the ground, the whole nine yards.
I'd bring my fingertips to my chapped, pursed lips
and cast the kiss like seeds through the hexagons of wire.
It probably doesn't seem like much, but it helped.

Crows skulked in my bare trees back then, heckled
in ¾ time with their stylish memes and billboard warnings:
*You will always attract what you fear! Have you grown too old
to be loved?* Still, every now and then, in the middle of an errand
or a frenzied set of jumping jacks, another voice broke in.
Even though I recognized it as my own, it was bolder
and more avant-garde than I'd ever been. It had the audacity
to proclaim there was nothing all that wrong with me. Said
I might be capable of astonishing things, even love. Assured me
you were out there somewhere, and would astonish me
with your love. It was an ancient voice, too, and tender,
as tender as your fingers were when you slowly, one by one,
untwisted the hexagons of chicken wire and let yourself in.

Reasons to Be Cheerful in an Age of Really Bad News

There are breach menders in the world
they advertise their expertise on the sides of trucks
There are tea kettles that moan like trains
Entire evenings that smell like rain
The county prison library is full of adult romance novels
with the last three pages torn out
Your heart is still versatile enough
to beat in that holy emptiness between your legs
Between earthworms & stars
us & us
Everything passes
Every blister runs out of fester & steam
All eras weep & fade
You've seen worse days
& better
You've heard
Maria Callas & Deep Purple shatter the same courtyard
under the same blue dome of morning
while at the other end of town
carpenters sang between hammer beats
about how pretty they are
You've lived
in a fungus lab, under a piano, by a river
Fellow travelers have wished you good courage
as you struggled through the square
under the weight of your hunger & your dreams
You've bought warm loaves of bread from strangers
& carried each one home in the crook of your arm
Cretan widows have left peanut butter jars
full of wildflowers on your doorstep
& in a laundromat somewhere not far from here
it's entirely possible
the naked accordionist hasn't been arrested yet
He could still be squeezing out polkas
to the beat of a load
while the other patrons
strip down to their underwear
& dance

Damnit, I'm already lying

when I call it paradise

the daffodil-yellow houseboat
we rose and fell on for two weeks in Puerto Rico

The hammock couldn't be trusted
the kayak had a bad leak

Every morning the million roosters
could have ground our coffee beans with their screams

But when I tell you we got used to all of it
you can believe me

It's kind of a postcard lie to say
we made some friends down there

unless you count the pelicans who studied us with their shy eyes
and Luis, our crabman neighbor in the junkyard dingy

who crooned in Spanglish about how much he loved us
whenever he got drunk

He clapped and did an elfin jig for us
when we barely paddled in from the storm

He praised our drowned hair and blistered fists
which he asked us to open

to receive the two broken-off pieces of coral he'd chosen
from the million broken-off pieces

His voice rose and fell
and splintered like the pier when he called out

But you only laugh and say goodbye! as we grinned at his antics
and backed away into our tidal kitchen

Rain sizzled through the eaves into our frying pan that night
while the packs of homeless dogs on shore

bellowed at the storm clouds and the stars above them
with equal bewilderment

We really did love him, in our way
We really did get used to all of it

The Vanishings

This morning I lost my mind
when I woke to geese flying so close to our tent
I could hear their wings whirring

and then their honks thrummed my ribcage
Too sleepy to put language to it
I became one of them

and flew upriver, away from my mind
which lay brooding on yesterday's yellowjacket sting
that almost choked the breath from me

along with the wildfires and floods
the disappearances of honeybees and democracies
and my memory

of what I came here for
Was it the knife or the glue?
Was I searching for severe storm warnings

or a good place to enter the river? When I lose my mind
my body wants to hatch like mayflies off the current
and float into the arms of trees

where the ones who make it
past the clear-eyed beaks of cedar waxwings
couple with the life force

They'll die as soon as they lay their eggs
on the river tonight, but they keep rising all day long
past my breast strokes and paddle pulls, my dread

treading water. If I stop to watch them long enough,
the next time lightning cracks and rain pummels earth
it won't matter when my mind crawls inside the tent

and zips the rainfly shut, waiting for the end: the high winds,
the five-trunked silver maple that mothers this island
finally torn from her roots and crushing us all. The rest of me

will keep breathing and make it past the waxwings
to couple with the claps of thunder, the bolts of fire
the burn of rapture, return, all I came here for

Some Skin

in response to Xaviera Simmons' video "Clap (For the Brothers)"

For the brothers, for the sisters, for the Other
For our fists unfolding, the palms of our hands coming together
Each pair of legs straddling the same planet as it whirls through space
For the shake, the jump rope revolution we make
with the hemp of our arms
Mine white, yours black, mine black, yours white
Our thumbs entwined
Each hair follicle and pore swollen open
by the heat of the same whirling sun
Our fists and wrists groping through the trumped-up news
that we were ever apart
Hello? Hello? Hello in there
Lifeline to lifeline
Veins blue and braided delivering the same news
to the lookalike knuckles knocking away
inside the cage of our ribs
Hello in there
Going deep, going beneath the spark that sparked the knock
Us recharging it now with our slaps and grips and knocks
Our rolling onward
Hey, come back
Hey brother, where you been?
Give me some skin

scrambled
> *after David Lerner*
> *for my brother Bill*

all i want to do is
return to my brother's San Francisco
where he tore down the steep streets on his bike
like burnt rain
all i want to do is teach the world to surround me
in my post-deathbed confoundment
but all i get is frightened footsteps
tiptoeing past the morgue

& i'd rather travel the world as Edvard Munch's *Scream*
than climb up into Emily Dickenson's prissy funeral carriage
i'd rather dine on the molded raspberries in your fridge
than sign your death certificate

i need to unscramble this mortal coil
need to put your bare dead feet to the floor
pack your rotting torso back inside your rib cage
& lead you to the phone

but this ain't no 911
no whiskey bottle of tears
no intoxicated handkerchief
this ain't no poem to wring out & drink

it is the very last teaspoonful of oatmeal
you will ever swallow
it is the very last spasm of self-hatred
you will ever have
it is all the homeless people you tended to in the Tenderloin
demanding to know where you went
asking how your life
could have been any more emptied out than theirs

i come not to bury you, brother, but to gather you up
not to find your last will & testament
or give away your worldly possessions
but to rifle through your journals
& read what you've left me
maybe one phrase of evidence
you finally broke through your turmoil
& became one with the oneness
you always swore was out there somewhere

because death is an excellent thing
surely we all need it
but there is even more we need to stay alive for these days
& anyway death is just life
gathering itself in the darkened womb of your fridge
the sparkling fur growing over your last bowl of oatmeal
the parched marigolds on your back steps going to seed

we still need you here, brother
because capitalism is still in fashion
& the mountainsides are still in flames
& the statue of Buddha on your windowsill
hasn't brought us any closer to home

but just like you always swore they would
the dead stars still keep offering up their light
if we keep offering up just one more breath

here's mine
where's yours

His Mother Still Speaks in the Present Tense
When She Speaks of Him

Tamir Rice is only 12 years old
and still into Batman
when those cops pull up to gun him down in the park,
and it's entirely possible
he's pretending to be a superhero
in the moment they take him down,
and you will too if two white cops
lurch out of their patrol car with their guns drawn
while you're pretending to be a superhero.
And you're black. And you love Curious George.
And you still get spooked by the scary movies
you watch with your older brother.
Remember? You play sports with a swagger,
can hit three-pointers on the court
when you dribble with the high-schoolers,
but you still have it in you
to crochet embroidery
for your mother, still crawl
into bed with her some nights
because some nights are harder to believe in
than superheroes when you're a black boy
in America. You don't care
if that Lego model airplane you crave
is for five year-olds—you want to fly
and you're going to fly.
You're going to be a superhero,
a cartoonist, the man who beats Lebron
at his own game. You're going to throw a football
with a spin so tight, it's still spiraling
through the skies of Cleveland today,
and none of us are going to snag it
without going down too.

How to Overcome the Burn of Cremation

Clip off a snippet of her hair
To tie into a snare for a fish
Promise her that when you finally catch this fish
You will kiss it on its gasping lips
And cast it back into the sea
Don't let it matter that her corpse no longer hears you
Or cares about the sea
Breathe
Breathe deep
Hold her stony hand
Stroke her petrified face
Memorize this indifference instead of her delight
Don't wonder what she's staring at—
Her comrades in the Memory Support Ward
Stared like this, too
Go ahead and joke with the cremator
She would love him
Funny, Irish, fluent as the Styx with good stories
If she were here, she could have delayed him with her own
But she's not here
So don't press your face to the glass in the viewing room
Don't let your eyes follow the cardboard box she's lying in
As it's conveyed like a grocery item
Or another good story
Into the fire

Homecoming

What do you call it, at dusk, after a long day's drive,
when you hurry your suitcase through the rain
and are pulled up short by thousands of fireflies in the yard,
gliding like gondolas among the glimmering drops?
What presses you, breathless and spattered, to call out *hello* to them
before you slip up the flagstones and step into your empty house?

Is it good manners, or longing? And what makes you remember,
as you crouch to unload your leftover road food into the fridge,
that you, too, are an animal? That for you, too, there's something
out in the downpour you might really need?
   Where does it come from,
this sudden premonition that you will live the rest of your life a fossil,
a hermetically sealed vessel, if you don't peel off your clothes,

kick off your shoes and step back outside? Look, whatever it is,
there's not enough of it in this world. Just go ahead
      and open the door.
The darkness is warm as mint, and the rain smells like stones.
Let yourself stand empty-handed among the fireflies. Who knows—
maybe nothing will happen. Maybe you'll feel like a fool. Or maybe
a drop of rain will buzz your nipple like the wing beat of a dove.

The smoky tang of a thundercloud could fall into your open mouth
and burn through all the things you never said or did.
   You might finally
understand that whoever it is you want to tell this to is gone.
And if this idea brings you to your knees, so be it.
Down here in the wet grass, where the fireflies are still blinking,
you could be, as far as anybody knows, kneeling in the stars.

What Happens When I Drive Long Distances

I press up the hill
take the curves like the daughter
of an oil tycoon
speed wind jitterbugging my scarf
& strumming my hair
as a song yowls from the speakers
& billows the map of the world
tacked up in my mind

White divider lines slide at me
like a threaded needle basting
asphalt to Earth

The superintendent of the road crew
reaches through the road fumes
to shake each worker's hand
while thoroughbreds swish their tails
& dip their heads to the beat

Each mile breeds more wonder
The trailer sagging with ivy
The guy on his porch wiping sleep from his eyes
The turkey vulture waiting above us

Everything is welcome
Even death

For each wrecked deer & bloated possum
I lay my hand over my heart
then pass them up to heaven
where the summer puffs of white
are also rolling through this world
as the smoke of burnt fossils
shimmies out my tailpipe
& the only brown woman in town
sweeps up at Mickey D's
& the cows sink to their knees
& Earth keeps on ticking beneath us

Making a Trade with the Abalone Shell Shaper

He told me it wouldn't be enough.
To be precise, he said
I don't think a little poem is going to do it for me, sister.
I was only 18 and curled up into myself
like last summer's petals,
but this pissed me off. I told him
What I'm going to write for you
won't be no 'little poem,' man.
He gazed across the Cascades to the Pacific,
considered the raw salt wind
and cliffs he'd had to climb
to find the multicolored shard
that now lay polished and necklaced
in my uncalloused palm. What on earth
could that hand do at this point?
Pick up a ballpoint pen from the drugstore
and doodle out a ditty about gulls dashing
rainbow tears against the rocks?
He studied my unchapped face and unbruised
bones, shaped his lips into an O
and shot a smoke ring over the valley.
How invisible he'd been in the fog,
how almost gone when his foot slipped on the cliff rock,
how inaudible his cry against the backdrop of the furious surf.
How faint life must have seemed in that moment,
yet how fiercely his heart beat,
and how audacious I was to convince him
that my little poem could hush those waves and make it sing.

In her time, writer **Katie Daley** has scrubbed the toilets of poets and mowed the fairways of gangsters. In between stints as a fruit picker, greenskeeper, sidewalk busker, motel maid, performer and teaching artist, she's written poems and essays that have appeared in publications such as *The Keepthings, Exposition Review, Hippocampus Magazine, Art Crimes, Slipstream, Times They Were A-Changing: Women Remember the '60s & '70s* (She Writes Press) and *After the Bell: Contemporary American Prose about School* (University of Iowa Press). She has performed her poetry across North America in theaters, radio broadcasts, ballrooms and junkyards. She is a recipient of three Individual Creativity Excellence Awards from the Ohio Arts Council and a fellowship at the Fine Arts Work Center in Provincetown, Massachusetts. Her audio productions include *Full Blast Alive: Voices from the Ruby* Side, a CD of her one-woman show, and *Zaggin' Like a Vagabond*, a marriage of spoken word, music and song by Drifters Inn, the band she formed with her husband. As a teaching artist, she does therapeutic writing outreach in drug rehabilitation programs, hospitals, schools and community centers throughout Northeast Ohio. Although poetry has long been her main squeeze, she's recently fallen in love with prose while writing a memoir about the hitchhiking, migrant-working journey she took in 1975 in the wake of her brother's suicide. *www.katiedaley.com*

www.ingramcontent.com/pod-product-compliance
Lightning Source LLC
Chambersburg PA
CBHW022104080426
42734CB00009B/1483